Nobby T[...]
to Wa[...]

by Darren & Julia Spence

This book belongs to:

_____

"Night night, Nobby!"

The Chocolate Labrador puppy settled down in his basket. His owner switched off the kitchen lights and shut the door. He heard the stairs creaking, and then it was quiet.

He should be going to sleep now. But something told Nobby it was not a night for sleep. He sniffed the air. Amongst the wafts of tonight's dinner and damp boots drying by the fire, there was something else – a whiff of magic.

It was a clear night, and the moon shone brightly through the kitchen window. Nobby looked across at the back door and the moonbeam falling on the dog flap.

He got out of his basket by the fire and crept across the shiny kitchen floor towards the door. He paused, wagged his tail with excitement then leapt through his dog flap.

He flew through the air for a few seconds, then tumbled in a heap onto something very soft and very cold.

Scrambling to his feet, Nobby saw that he had landed by a hedge in a snowy field.

At first, it seemed as if there was no one about, but then he heard someone shouting and whistling. It seemed to be coming from the other side of the hedge.

He was too small to see over the hedge, but he soon found a gap and squeezed through. At the top of the field, he could see the man who was doing the whistling and shouting.

"Away! Away! Nell! Come by!"

At the bottom of the field was a flock of sheep moving towards a wooden pen.

Running along behind the sheep was a shaggy black and white dog. The dog darted this way and that, and now and then she would freeze, all the while watching the sheep.

Little by little, the flock drew closer to the pen. The dog guided them through the gate, then lay down beside it. Then the whistling man came running down the field and shut the gate. He bent down and spoke to the dog, but Nobby was too far away to hear what he said.

As the man walked on down the field, the shaggy dog glanced round. Her sharp eyes spotted Nobby immediately, and she bounded towards him.

"Hello," said Nobby.

"Oh, you're a dog!" said the dog.

"Er, yes," said Nobby. "What did you think I was?"

"A sheep, of course," said the other dog.

"What?!" exclaimed Nobby, a little put out at being mistaken for a sheep.

"Well, it's just that I'm looking for a sheep. We've lost one, you see. And being covered in snow like that, you looked – sheepish, like."

Nobby shook himself hard, and the snow on his back flew off in a shower.

"Ah, you're a Chocolate Labrador, aren't you?" said the other dog. "Are you lost?"

"Not exactly," said Nobby. "I'm Nobby, and I'm not lost, just visiting."

"Is that a fact?" said the dog. "Well, I'm Nell, but as you see Nobby, I'm a working sheepdog, and right now my job is to go and find the missing sheep. So if you'll excuse me …"

And she started back down the hill.

"Wait!" said Nobby, running after her. "I'll come and help."

Nell looked at him doubtfully, then said, "All right, then. You'll have to keep up, though. We'll start in the farmyard. She may have wandered into one of the outbuildings there."

NOBBY TRAVELS TO WALES

Nell led the way down to the farmyard. At one side stood an old stone farmhouse; at the other was an enormous barn with a blue and yellow tractor parked in front.

"I'll search the barn," said Nell, "you look around the yard."

Nobby peered into all the small buildings and sheds and pushed his nose into all the dusty corners, but the sheep was nowhere to be seen. He trotted over to the barn to wait for Nell by the tractor.

Hang on a minute. There was something moving in the cab! Nobby put his front paws up against the tractor and gave a gentle 'woof'. He jumped back smartly as a squawking feathery bundle hurtled out of the cab and onto the ground.

It was a little brown hen. She clucked indignantly at Nobby.

Nobby peered into the cab once more – just to check – and there on the seat was a smooth, brown egg.

At that moment, Nell came out of the barn.

"Ah, broody hen, is it?" she said. "You find them laying in all sorts of places. Come on. We'll try the cow shed."

Nell led the way to a large shed full of cows, all munching contentedly.

"They've just come back from milking," explained Nell.

There were plenty of cows – but no sheep. As Nobby followed Nell out, he felt his paws sink into something squelchy.

"Oh, and mind the cow pats!" barked Nell.

Next they went over to some large pens that turned out to be full of pale pink pigs. There were plenty of pigs – but no sheep.

"She must be in one of the fields," said Nell. "We'll have to go up the hillside."

The little search party made its way up the hillside, looking in every field and along every hedgerow. As they neared the top, Nobby was surprised to see a large, black hole in the hillside. "What's that?" he asked.

"It's a cave," said Nell. "Well, it's an old slate mine really, but it's not used now. We'd better have a look inside though – just in case."

But then something made both dogs stop in their tracks. Drifting from the dark mouth of the cave was a wisp of smoke.

Nobby looked anxiously at Nell. "What's that?" he asked, again.

"Well now, there's a thing. I don't really know," said Nell. "But I think we still need to have a look."

Nobby followed Nell into the cave. As his eyes got used to the smoky darkness, he noticed something in the corner. It was moving. It was definitely an animal, it looked about the size of a sheep.

They edged closer. The smoke cleared a little, and Nobby saw an animal unlike any he had ever seen before. It had leathery skin, a long snout, a long, snake-like tail and – wings!"

"What's that?" he whispered.

"It's … it's a dragon!" said Nell in a very surprised voice. "At least, it looks like a dragon, and it's smoking like a dragon. But – dragons aren't real. You only get dragons in stories, see."

"Not real?" said the dragon. "Well, in that case, you won't mind if I do this." He opened his mouth and let out a blast of orange and yellow fire. Nell and Nobby only just managed to dodge the flames.

"Maybe I was mistaken," said Nell hastily.

The dragon looked satisfied. "That's how it is with most people," it said, with a hint of sadness. "There aren't many of us left now, you see. I'm the only one this side of the Beacons."

"I don't wish to seem rude, said Nell, cautiously, "but you seem quite – er, small. I thought dragons were bigger."

"They are!" said the dragon. "That is to say, I will be, when I'm fully grown. I'm only five hundred years old. I'll be three times this size when I reach a thousand."

Nobby thought what a good thing it was that the dragon was only a young one. Then he suddenly remembered why they were there, and he had an idea.

"Excuse me," he said slightly nervously. "But we are trying to find a lost sheep and we were hoping …"

"Oh, well you'd better go and look for it," said the dragon.

"But the thing is," said Nobby, not to be put off, "we've looked everywhere, and now we need some help. And I couldn't help noticing your wings – you can fly, can't you?"

"Of course I can fly!" said the dragon.

"Well," said Nobby, "I wonder if you might fly over the hillside and see if you can see the lost sheep."

The dragon looked rather reluctant, but said that it might.

Nell looked at Nobby in admiration.

Nobby and Nell stood outside the mouth of the cave and watched as the dragon spread its enormous wings and soared high over the snowy countryside.

It flew in circles, getting further and further away from the cave until it was a tiny red speck against the grey sky.

After a few minutes, the speck disappeared completely and Nobby wondered if that was the last they would see of the grumpy dragon.

They waited and waited. Nobby kept moving his paws in case they got frozen to the ground. Then, just when he thought they should give up, the speck reappeared. A few seconds later, the dragon landed in front of the cave.

"There's a sheep in the snowdrift at the edge of the road down there," it said. "Now if you'll excuse me …"

"But there are lots of snowdrifts by the road," said Nell. "Please, would you be so good as to show us which one?"

Again, the dragon looked a little reluctant, but said that it would. It spread its wings and glided down the hill, and the two dogs scampered after.

When the dogs reached the road, they had to go only a little way before they caught up with the dragon. It was standing by a particularly large snowdrift. Sticking out of the snow was the head of a very miserable-looking sheep.

"Thank you," said Nell to the dragon. Then she looked worried. "However are we going to get her out?"

Nobby had an idea.

"Excuse me," he said to the dragon, "but you can breathe fire, can't you? So I wonder if you could melt the snowdrift with your breath?"

The dragon sighed rather heavily, but said that it could.

It started to breathe very softly on the snow. This time the flames that came out were much smaller and as they licked the snow, it began to melt. Soon the whole snowdrift was turning to water and before long the sheep was free.

"Thank you," said Nell.

"Don't mention it," said the dragon, briskly. It spread its wings, and was gone.

"Are all dragons like that?" Nobby asked Nell.

"I don't know," said Nell. "Anyway, we'd best be getting this sheep back. Look, it's starting to snow again."

They set off down the road, Nell driving the sheep in front of her and Nobby following a little way behind so as not to confuse the sheep.

The snow was falling more heavily now, and Nobby found that the snowflakes were getting in his eyes. He tried to watch where Nell was going, but she kept disappearing.

Then Nobby realised that he couldn't see Nell at all. He wasn't even sure he was going in the right direction.

He stopped. "Nell! Where are you?" he barked.

He thought he heard Nell's reply coming from somewhere over to the right. He started walking again, but a few steps later he bumped into something hard and he felt himself being covered by a blanket of thick snow.

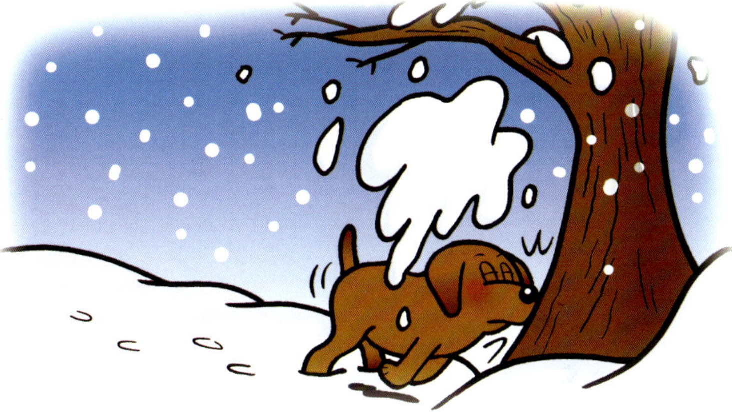

The snow felt soft, but
not at all cold. It had a
familiar woolly smell.

Nobby opened his eyes and saw that it wasn't snow at all. He was underneath his own fluffy dog blanket in his own comfortable basket. Nobby settled himself back on top of his blanket, put his head between his paws and fell asleep.

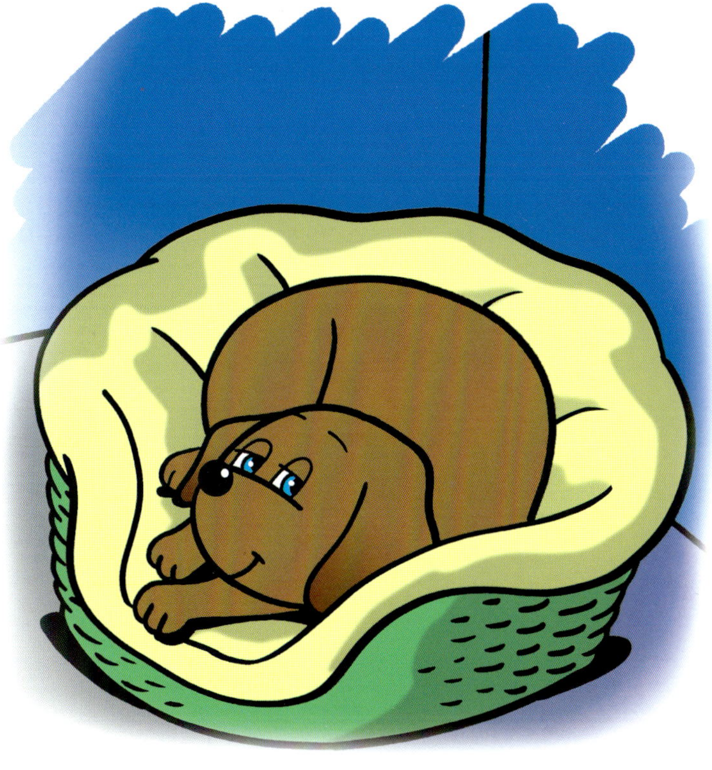

"Morning, Nobby!"

Nobby's owner breezed into the kitchen and flung open the curtains, letting the warm sunshine flood the kitchen.

She walked over to Nobby's basket and bent down to ruffle the fur on his back.

"Nobby!" she exclaimed. "Whatever has happened to your tail?"

Nobby turned his sleepy head to look. The tip of his tail appeared to be slightly singed.

He looked back at his owner apologetically and wagged his tail, to show that it was all right.

"Hmm," said his owner, "What have you been doing? Sitting too close to the fire?"

NOBBY TRAVELS TO WALES

Facts about **Wales** ...

Capital City:	**Cardiff**
Money:	**£ Pound Sterling**
Welsh Dog:	**Border Collie**
Popular Food:	**Welsh Rarebit**
Languages Spoken:	**Welsh, English**
Flying Time from London, England:	**25 Minutes**

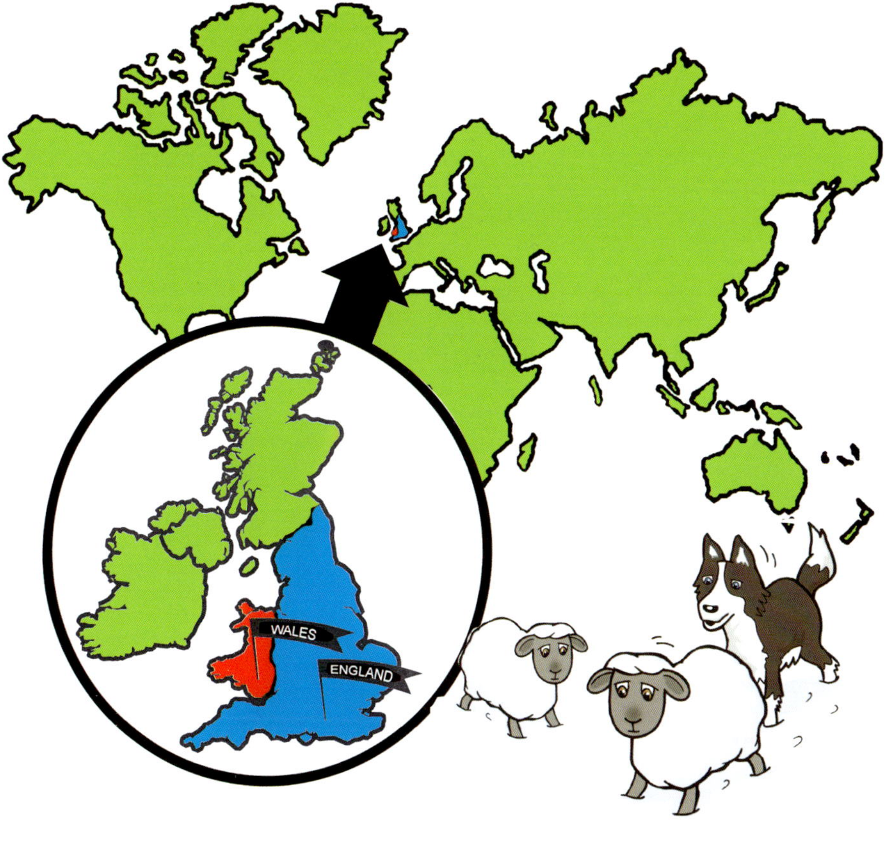
WALES
ENGLAND

NOBBY TRAVELS TO WALES

Become a Nobby Traveller !

If you enjoyed this "Nobby Travels" story, why not join our exclusive members club and become a Nobby Traveller? When you join, you'll receive:

- ★ a Nobby Traveller passport to record your travels
- ★ a Nobby Traveller bag
- ★ a set of Nobby Travels stickers
- ★ Money-off vouchers

... **plus**, you'll have access to the members-only area of the Nobby Travels website, where you can:

- ★ download loads of cool stuff
- ★ take part in competitions
- ★ keep up to date with news about Nobby

To become a Nobby Traveller, simply visit www.nobbytravels.com/nobbytraveller

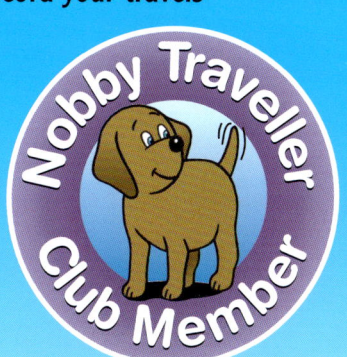

All for just £5 per year

Nobby Traveller Club Member

NOBBY TRAVELS TO WALES